NAPLAN* Skills Handbook

This is not an officially endorsed publication of the NAPLAN program and is produced by Amba Press independently of Australian governments

YEAR 5 TESTS PREPARATION GUIDE

5

Published in 2025 by Amba Press, Melbourne, Australia
www.ambapress.com.au

© Kilbaha Education 2025

This is not an officially endorsed publication of the NAPLAN program and is produced by Amba Press independently of Australian governments.

All rights reserved. No part of this book may be reproduced or transmitted in any form or by any means, electronic or mechanical, including photocopying, recording or by any information storage and retrieval system, without prior permission in writing from the publisher.

Cover design: Tess McCabe
Editor: Rica Dearman

ISBN: 9781923215924 (pbk)
ISBN: 9781923215931 (ebk)

A catalogue record for this book is available from the National Library of Australia.

Contents

Introduction	1
What to expect	3
Revising for NAPLAN	5
Using this book	7
Test days tips	9
Writing test	11
Reading test	16
Language conventions test	35
Numeracy test	46
Answers	59

Introduction

What is NAPLAN?

NAPLAN (National Assessment Program – Literacy and Numeracy) is a national test that all Australian students in Years 3, 5, 7 and 9 take each year. Think of it as a way to check how well you're doing with important skills like writing, reading, and maths.

What is the purpose of NAPLAN?

NAPLAN helps you, your parents and your teachers understand how you're progressing with these essential skills. It's like a checkpoint to make sure you're on track with your learning and to identify any areas where you might need extra support.

What is being assessed?

NAPLAN tests four main areas:

- Writing (either a narrative or persuasive piece)
- Reading comprehension
- Language conventions (spelling, grammar and punctuation)
- Numeracy (maths and problem-solving)

How is it graded?

Your answers are marked either electronically (for multiple choice) or by trained markers (for writing and text entries). The tests are designed to adjust to your level – if you do well, you'll get harder questions; if you find them tricky, you'll get questions better matched to your level.

What results are provided?

You'll get a detailed report showing how you performed in each area. It shows your individual achievement and how you compare to other students in your year level across Australia.

Why is NAPLAN important?

NAPLAN is important for schools, the government and education planning, but for you personally, it's just one test on one day – it won't affect your grades, high school graduation or future opportunities, so try your best, but don't stress too much about it.

What to expect?

What tests are involved?

You'll complete four different tests:
- Writing
- Reading
- Language conventions
- Numeracy (with both calculator and non-calculator sections)

Why is NAPLAN online?

The online format makes the test more personalised to your ability level. It's also faster to get results and includes helpful features like being able to flag questions to review later.

When, what and how?

- Tests happen at school in March
- You'll use a computer or tablet
- Each test has a different time limit
- You can use a ruler but you are not allowed to use blocks, calculators or other mathematical tools during the test
- You can flag questions to come back to later

How does the timer work in NAPLAN online?

The test screen shows a timer that counts down how much time is left. You can choose to hide or show this timer during most of the test, but in the last five minutes, the timer will automatically appear to let you know time is nearly up.

How do audio parts of the test work?

You'll need headphones for some parts of the test, especially for spelling questions and maths problems. The test includes audio that reads out the writing task and other sections to help you understand them better.

Revising for NAPLAN

Why revise for NAPLAN?

Practising helps you feel more confident and comfortable with the test format. When you're familiar with the types of questions, you can focus on showing what you know rather than worrying about how the test works.

How to revise?

There are many ways to revise. Try some of these:

- Practise similar questions
- Get familiar with the online format using the public demonstration site
- Review topics you find challenging
- Try different question types
- Practise managing your time
- Conduct trial tests

Why do trial tests?

Trial tests help you:

- Get used to the test format
- Practise time management
- Identify areas where you might need more practice
- Feel more confident on test day

Do the tests in this book match those in NAPLAN online?

The questions are similar in style and difficulty to what you'll see in NAPLAN, but remember that the actual online test will adjust to your performance level as you go.

Using this book

How is this book organised?

Each section focuses on one test area (writing, reading, language or numeracy) and includes:

- Practice questions
- Example answers
- Tips and strategies
- Explanations of different question types

Each student in Australia takes the NAPLAN tests in the same order:

Day 1: Writing

Day 2: Reading

Day 3: Conventions of language (grammar, punctuation, spelling)

Day 4: Numeracy

How should you use this book?

There are many ways you can use it:

- Start with areas you find most challenging
- Complete the practice tests under timed conditions
- Review your answers and understand any mistakes
- Use the online practice tests to get familiar with the computer format
- Take breaks between practice sessions
- Keep track of topics you need to review more

Test days tips

How to prepare for test days?

Here are some other ways you can prepare for the NAPLAN tests:
- Get a good sleep the night before
- Have a healthy breakfast
- Arrive at school on time
- Bring your water bottle
- Make sure you have the equipment you need (like headphones)
- Download and install the NAPLAN Locked Down browser
- Go to the toilet before the test starts
- Take some slow, deep breaths to stay calm

What happens if you are sick on one of the test days?

Don't worry! If you're sick on test day, stay home and get better. Your school will arrange for you to do the test on another day during the NAPLAN test window. There are catch-up tests available for students who are absent during the main testing period.

What happens if you don't feel you did well on the day?

Remember that NAPLAN is just one test on one day – it's not a pass or fail test. Everyone has good days and bad days. Your teachers look at lots of different ways to assess how you're going at school, not just NAPLAN. If you're worried about your performance, talk to your parents or teachers about it. They can help explain your results when they arrive and provide support if needed.

Stressed? Nervous? Anxious?

Here are some techniques you could use if you feel stressed or nervous during the actual test:

- Take slow, deep breaths – breathe in for four counts, hold for four, breathe out for four
- Remember you can flag difficult questions and come back to them later
- Have a quick stretch in your chair
- Take a sip of water
- Close your eyes for a moment if you need to
- Focus on one question at a time rather than thinking about the whole test
- Remind yourself that you've prepared well and are doing your best
- Use positive self-talk like *I can do this* or *I'll try my best*

Writing test

You have 42 minutes to complete the writing test, which includes:

- 2 minutes for reading/listening to stimulus
- 5 minutes for planning
- 30 minutes for writing
- 5 minutes for editing

Total: 42 minutes

You will be provided with a 'writing stimulus' or 'prompt' – an idea or topic – and asked to write a response of a particular text type (genre). The stimulus will be read aloud to all students.

In the NAPLAN test you will write a narrative OR a persuasive piece of writing.

We have provided one test example of each style and some suggestions to keep in mind for each one.

You are to type your answer online but can prepare or plan your response with a pen/pencil and paper.

Tips for writing a good narrative or story

Start strong
- Tell us who is in your story
- Tell us where and when it happens
- Make it interesting from the start

Make your story exciting
- Have something interesting happen
- Make your characters do things
- Tell us how they feel
- Use words that paint pictures

End well
- Solve any problems in your story
- Don't just say 'I woke up' or 'The End'
- Make sure all parts of your story fit together

Remember to:
- Write neatly between the lines
- Leave spaces between words
- Use capital letters and full stops
- Check your spelling
- Read your story back to make sure it makes sense

The Note

Today you are going to write a narrative or story.

The idea for your story is 'The Note'.

What will be written on the note? Why is it attached to the $5?

Who is writing the note? Who is receiving the note?

What will happen if the paper clip falls off?

Think about:

- The characters and where they are
- The complication or problem to be solved
- How the story will end

Remember to:

- Consider everything in the picture – even small details can give you great ideas for your story!
- Plan your story before you start
- Write in sentences
- Pay attention to the words you choose, your spelling and punctuation, and paragraphs
- Check and edit your writing when you have finished

Tips for writing a good persuasive piece

Start strong
- Tell us what you think straight away
- Make your opinion clear
- Let readers know why this matters

Give good reasons
- Use 'because' to explain your reasons
- Give examples
- Tell us why your idea is good
- Use words like 'should' and 'must'

End well
- Remind us of your opinion
- Sum up your main reasons
- Make your ending strong

Remember to:
- Write neatly between the lines
- Use capital letters and full stops
- Check your spelling
- Read your work back to check it makes sense
- Use joining words like 'because', 'and', 'also'

Cats or Dogs

Today you are going to write a persuasive piece.

A cat makes a better pet than a dog.

What do you think about this idea? Write to convince a reader of your opinions.

Think about:

- If you agree or disagree or see both sides of the argument
- An introduction – a way to introduce your ideas by clearly saying what you think about the topic
- Your opinions – with reasons or evidence that explain them
- A conclusion – a summary of the main points of your argument

Remember to:

- Plan your writing
- Write in sentences
- Pay attention to your spelling and punctuation
- Choose your words carefully to convince a reader of your opinions
- Use a new paragraph for each new idea
- Check and edit your writing so that it is clear for a reader

Reading test

This is a reading test.

There are 35 questions.

You have 45 minutes to complete the reading test.

In this test you will need to read each text, then read each question and choose the correct answer.

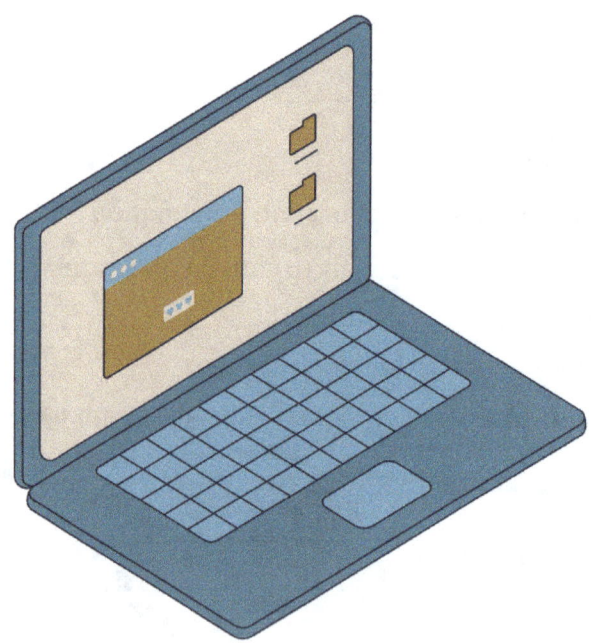

Read *The ant and the dove* and then answer questions 1 to 6.

The ant and the dove

By Phil Zinc

A tiny ant, having worked hard all day building his nest, was parched. He stood on the bank of a river and bent down to take a drink. The edge of the bank was slick and the ant slipped into the water. A solitary dove circled in the sky above and saw the ant in the river below, floundering for his life. The dove, being a kind creature, deftly flew across to the nearest tree, plucked a small twig from a branch and dropped it into the water for the ant to grasp a hold. The ant, clutching on to the twig, was then able to kick across to the bank and pull himself up out of the river.

Grateful for his life, the ant looked up to the sky to thank his saviour and noticed a man standing next to him, taking aim at the dove with a bow and arrow. The ant swiftly bit the man on his toe, causing the man to jump in pain and shoot the arrow far away from the dove.

The ant and the dove questions 1 to 6.

1. **What word could be used to describe the bank of the river instead of *slick*?**
   - o   dry
   - o   slippery
   - o   sticky
   - o   grassy

2. **What word best describes the dove in this story?**
   - o   coward
   - o   hero
   - o   bully
   - o   tease

3. **Why did the ant bite the man on the toe?**
   - o   the man made the ant fall in the river
   - o   the ant was afraid
   - o   the ant did not like people
   - o   the ant wanted to save the dove

4. **In the beginning of the story, what word could best be used in place of *parched*?**
   - o   angry
   - o   refreshed
   - o   thirsty
   - o   cool

5. **In the story, the ant is *'floundering for his life'*. This means the ant is**
   - o   running for his life
   - o   fighting with the dove
   - o   fighting with the man
   - o   trying not to drown

6. **What do you think is the message to be taken from this story?**
   - o   kind acts are repaid
   - o   ants can drown
   - o   men do not like doves
   - o   rivers are dangerous

Read *Orangutan* and then answer questions 7 to 12.

Orangutan
By Ron Thomas & Shirley Sydenham

Orangutans are great apes. They are found in the forests of Sumatra and Kalimantan. They have long, shaggy, reddish-brown hair. Males are usually larger than females, weigh about 75 kilograms and stand about 1.4 metres tall. Orangutans are arboreal, which means they live in trees, feeding on fruit, leaves, bark, birds' eggs, ants and other insects. They build platforms of woven branches for sleeping. Females sometimes live in small groups of three or four, but the males are largely solitary animals. Orangutans live a fairly nomadic life, travelling about as they search for food. Females rarely come down from the trees, but males sometimes travel along the ground.

After mating, females are pregnant for about nine months. They give birth to usually one, but sometimes two, young.

Orangutans are endangered because their forest habitats are being destroyed, and because they have been hunted and sold as pets. Humans are their only enemy. It is estimated that there are only about 25,000 left in the wild.

Rehabilitation centres have been set up in Sumatra and Kalimantan in an attempt to save Asia's only great ape. Here, orangutans that have been kept in captivity as pets are taught the skills needed to survive in the wild. The animals are studied and treated for illness. The rehabilitation centres encourage visitors as part of a program to raise awareness about these endangered animals.

Orangutan questions 7 to 12.

7. **The text describes orangutans as *arboreal*. This means that orangutans**
   - ○ live in caves
   - ○ live in captivity
   - ○ live in trees
   - ○ are not real

8. **Male orangutans**
   - ○ live in groups
   - ○ stay in the trees
   - ○ like to be alone
   - ○ weigh about 100 kilograms

9. **Orangutans are an *endangered* species. This means that orangutans**
   - ○ are dangerous
   - ○ are kept in captivity
   - ○ are in danger
   - ○ are destroying the forests

10. **In Sumatra and Kalimantan some orangutans are kept in rehabilitation centres. They are kept in these centres**
    - ○ to be sold later as pets
    - ○ to learn to be nomadic
    - ○ to learn survival skills
    - ○ to protect the forest

11. **Orangutans do *not* eat**
    - leaves
    - birds' eggs
    - insects
    - birds

12. **Which of the following statements about orangutans is *incorrect***
    - males usually weigh more than females
    - females usually stay up in the trees
    - they only have one enemy
    - females usually give birth to more than one young

Read *Australian drought* and then answer questions 13 to 18.

Australian drought

15 June

Dear Editor,

Our country is experiencing the worst drought in its history. Farmers are struggling to keep their crops and their livestock alive. We need to manage our water resources as carefully as possible and treat water like it is gold, before it all runs out.

It makes me so angry when I see people wasting water, using it to wash things like the outsides of their houses or their cars when they should be using grey water from their washing machines to do these things. Better yet, they should be using rainwater tanks.

I don't think the Government is doing enough. I think the Government should provide every house in Australia with a water tank, so that every household can use rainwater wherever they can instead of using precious drinking water from their taps for everything.

We all need to be more conscious of our environment.

Patty Wilkins

22 June

Dear Editor,

I agree with Patty Wilkins' letter (15 June) in that all Australians need to be conserving water and that we need to be conscious of our environment.

I don't think she has a right to be angry at people, though. People pay a lot of money for their cars and cars need to be washed so that they can be protected from damaging bird droppings that can eat away at the paint. But I do agree that recycled water and rainwater should be used.

Our Government has put plenty of restrictions on the use of water such as only allowing people to water plants two days per week and only prior to eight o'clock in the morning.

Also, anyone who buys a rainwater tank can claim money back from the Government to cover some of the costs.

I also don't think there are many people being water 'Wallys'. Most people are doing their best to save water wherever they can.

Bill Freedman

Australian drought questions 13 to 18.

13. **Where does grey water come from?**
    - ○ taps
    - ○ rainwater tanks
    - ○ washing machines
    - ○ gutters

14. **Which of the following do the two writers disagree on?**
    - ○ water needs to be conserved
    - ○ the Government is doing enough
    - ○ the environment is precious
    - ○ rainwater tanks help in a drought

15. **Bill writes that the Government has '*put plenty of restrictions on the use of water*'. Why does he write this?**
    - ○ he agrees with Patty
    - ○ he works for the Government
    - ○ he disagrees with Patty
    - ○ he thinks that Australians are water 'Wallys'

16. **Why does Patty think that water tanks are a great idea?**
    - ○ so people will use less grey water
    - ○ so people will use more tap water
    - ○ so people can get money back from the Government
    - ○ so people will use more rainwater

17. **What does Patty's letter tell us about Patty?**
    - she likes the Government
    - she cares for the environment
    - she cares for Bill
    - she is not a farmer

18. **What type of letter is Bill's?**
    - a comment
    - an instruction
    - a response
    - a list

Read *Eggs* and then answer questions 19 to 24.

Eggs

By Aoife Bearsley

Thomas isn't back with the eggs yet, but my feet are burning, so I lay the towel out next to the tin on the concrete and sit in the middle of it. I want to be in the shade but Thomas reckons the tin has to be in the full sun.

It will get hot enough. The sun is about as close to the Earth as it can get on days like today. It's like a big orange ball up there and down here everything is tinged with yellow. All the leaves on the trees kind of sparkle and those 'birches' Mum loves so much look a bit sick on days like today, with the tops of them tipping over toward the ground like they're looking for something to drink.

The back door squeaks and a few seconds later Thomas tiptoes down the drive, staying in the strip of shade next to the house. 'They're straight from the fridge,' he whispers, 'so they should sizzle really well.'

'Was your dad up?' I ask, but I know he wasn't, because Thomas wouldn't have gone inside for the eggs if his dad was awake. He would have snuck up back to the chook shed instead.

'No. He did a late shift last night, so I reckon it should be at least three o'clock before I have to go in.' Thomas sits and grins, drawing two speckled eggs out from his pocket and places them down between us on the towel.

He splays his hand out over the tin lid, not touching it, but very close. He presses a fingertip down on the lid and then rips his hand back toward his chest. 'Wow, mate!' he cackles, 'that feels hot enough to cook a steak on!' He inspects his finger and shows it to me. It's bright red on the tip. I laugh. He plucks an egg from the towel and I do the same. We sit grinning at one another for a moment, holding our eggs next to the rim of the tin.

Thomas counts to three and we both crack our eggs, splitting their hard bellies open and pouring their guts out onto the lid. The eggs slide and wobble a bit, but their clear jelly bodies start to turn a wispy, milky white...

Eggs questions 19 to 24.

19. **Why would Thomas have gone up to the chook shed instead of the house?**

    ○ to get out of the sun

    ○ because his dad wouldn't catch him stealing eggs from there

    ○ to hide from the narrator

    ○ for extra eggs

20. **What does the narrator mean by the sentence '...*It will get hot enough*'?**

    _____

    _____

21. **'...*their clear jelly bodies start to turn a wispy, milky white...*' What does this mean?**

    ○ Thomas and the narrator are turning white

    ○ the sun is going down

    ○ the eggs are cooking

    ○ the eggs are rotten

22. **In the story, Thomas' dad did a late shift the night before, so Thomas thinks he has until at least three o'clock before he has to go in. This suggests that Thomas**

    ○ needs to go in before the sun goes down

    ○ needs to go in before his dad wakes up

    ○ knows that his dad will not be angry

    ○ will get into trouble if he goes to the chook shed

23. **What kind of word *best* describes the relationship between Thomas and the narrator?**
    - o brothers
    - o enemies
    - o friends
    - o cousins

24. **Why do you think the narrator laughs when Thomas shows off his burnt finger?**
    - o because he is hot
    - o because he wants Thomas to be hurt
    - o because he doesn't like Thomas
    - o because he is amazed

Read *Water baby* and then answer questions 25 to 30.

Water baby

By Kirsty Murray

When the starting gun went off, Shane cut the water like a knife. She knew she was swimming well – she felt light and smooth. The water seemed to rush past beneath her. All her movements were precise, her arm stroke exact and powerful. The other competitors didn't have a chance. She took the lead and held it for the entire race.

When Shane climbed out of the pool and mounted the podium to receive her gold medal, she became the youngest Australian Olympic medallist in history. She was 15 years old…

Shane Elizabeth Gould was born in Sydney on 23 November 1956. She loved the water from babyhood. When bathtime was over, she cried to get back in the water. Before she was three she could swim underwater at the pool with her eyes open, and at five she was snorkelling around the reefs of Fiji. By the time she was 15 years old, she held every women's world freestyle record from 100m to 1,500m.

Shane had the perfect physique for a swimmer – tall and slim with wide shoulders and narrow hips. By the time she was 13, she knew that her gift for swimming was something special – she gave up all other interests and gave herself over to competitive swimming. She set her alarm for early-morning training, watched her diet and kept a logbook of her training routines. Her persistence and single-mindedness paid off. Between April 1971 and January 1972, she set seven new world records. By July 1972, she was so confident that she'd win gold at the Games that she asked her parents if she could have her braces removed just for the competition. She knew the cameras would be flashing and she wanted to look her best.

Shane Gould won three gold, one silver and a bronze medal at the 1972 Olympics.

Water baby questions 25 to 30.

25. **When the starting gun went off, Shane *'cut the water like a knife'*. This means that Shane**

    o   used a knife to cut the water

    o   dove into the water roughly

    o   went through the water sharply

    o   swam very slowly

26. **The text states that Shane *'gave herself over to competitive swimming'*. This means that she**

    o   gave up going to school

    o   gave up her diet

    o   brought herself over to the swimming pool

    o   gave up other activities for swimming

27. **Shane swam open-eyed underwater**

    o   during bathtime

    o   by age three

    o   while snorkelling

    o   by age five

28. **The main purpose of this text is to**

    o   instruct

    o   criticise

    o   argue

    o   inform

29. **Which quote from the text best shows that Shane was very determined to succeed?**
    - ○ *'she knew her gift for swimming was special'*
    - ○ *'she was so confident she'd win'*
    - ○ *'her persistence and single-mindedness paid off'*
    - ○ *'she loved the water from babyhood'*

30. **Why did Shane ask for her braces to be removed before the Olympics?**
    - ○ because they were slowing her down
    - ○ because she was confident she was going to win
    - ○ because she didn't like her photo being taken
    - ○ because she was persistent

Read *Elephants* and then answer questions 31 to 35.

Elephants

Elephants are the largest land mammals in the world. There are two species of elephant left: the **Asian** elephant (***Elephas maximus***) and the **African** elephant (***Loxodonta africana***). There are several differences between these two types of elephants.

At a height of 3 to 4 metres and weighing up to 7 tonnes, the African elephant is larger than the Asian elephant, which stands at a smaller 2 to 3.5 metres and can weigh up to 5 tonnes.

In addition, the Asian elephant has a large domed head and much smaller ears than the African elephant.

Female elephants, or *cows*, can reproduce up until they are 50 years old, with 2.5 to 4 years between births. Cows generally only give birth to a single calf, but in very rare cases can produce twins. Female elephants live in matriarchal groups in which one elder female is the leader.

Elephants are herbivores that typically eat all kinds of vegetation such as grasses, leaves, bark and fruit.

Both male and female African elephants have tusks. Only the male Asian elephants have tusks. Female Asian elephants have *tushes* – tiny little tusks that jut out just beyond their lips or some of the females have no tushes at all.

Elephants and their ecosystem

Elephants can have a very positive effect on their ecosystem. Elephants in the wild often live in very dry habitats. Their weight creates depressions in the ground that become precious traps for rainfall. With their powerful tusks and trunks they dig water holes in dry beds that are frequently used by other animals. Sometimes the water holes are the only source of water during the dry season. Because of their size, elephants also make pathways through dense scrub and forest for many other creatures to travel through.

Elephants questions 31 to 35.

31. **How do other animals in the ecosystem rely on elephants?**
    - ○ for protection
    - ○ as a water source
    - ○ as a provider of food
    - ○ for shelter

32. **Using information in the text, what is *a matriarchal group* likely to mean?**

    _____

    _____

33. **African and Asian elephants have different technical names: *Elephas maximus* and *Loxodonta africana*. Why is this?**
    - ○ they are different species
    - ○ they live on different sides of the world
    - ○ they are not similar in any way
    - ○ because African elephants are bigger

34. **From reading the text, we can tell that *herbivores***
    - ○ are *Loxodonta africana*
    - ○ do not eat meat
    - ○ have *tushes*
    - ○ give birth to a single calf

35. **What are some of the features of the Asian elephant?**

    _____

    _____

Language conventions test

This is the language conventions test (which covers spelling, grammar and punctuation).

There are 50 questions.

You have 45 minutes to complete the language conventions test.

There will be a mix of question types including:

- Multiple choice
- Short answer
- Error identification/correction
- Fill in the blank/missing word

The test typically starts with spelling questions before moving into grammar and punctuation. You need to identify errors and show your understanding of correct language usage through these various question formats.

Spelling

The spelling mistakes in these sentences have been circled. Write the correct spelling for each circled word in the box.

1. Jenna went (shoping) today.

    1. ☐

2. We waited (abowt) an hour for the bus.

    2. ☐

3. He used a ruler to (mesure.)

    3. ☐

4. Liz cut out the picture with her (sizzors.)

    4. ☐

5. Possums like eating (froot.)

    5. ☐

6. Everyone thinks Anna is (pritty.)

    6. ☐

7. Brendon loves Vegemite (samwiches.)

    7. ☐

8. Peter was (greatful) for his birthday present.

    8. ☐

9. Mrs Hartley is a good (teecher).

9. _____

10. Mum cooked a (sosage) on the barbecue.

10. _____

**The spelling mistakes on these labels have been circled.
Write the correct spelling for each circled word in the box.**

11. (cumputer) screen

11. _____

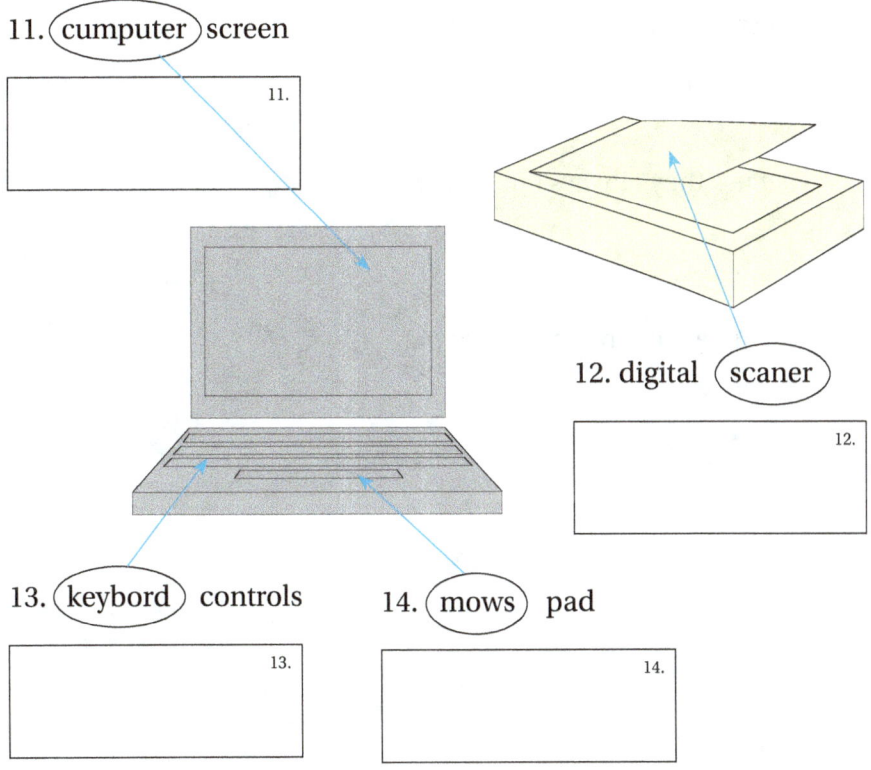

12. digital (scaner)

12. _____

13. (keybord) controls

13. _____

14. (mows) pad

14. _____

Read the text about *The visit*.

Each line has one word that is incorrectly spelled. Write the correct spelling of the word in the box.

The visit

15. My parrents have been waiting

16. a very long time for my unkle to

17. visit us. They allways talk about him

18. and are exited to see him again.

Each sentence has one word that is incorrect.
Write the correct spelling of the word in the box.

19. We need to show caushun when crossing the road.

19.

20. I am very good at rapping presents.

20.

21. My grandmother owns an expensive cristal ball.

21.

22. The art galery has many famous paintings.

22.

23. John claims he has the bigest feet in the school.

23.

24. The tourist lost his luggidge at the airport.

24.

25. Too much moishture in a home can cause mould.

25.

26. The mountain's summit was at a great hite.

26.

Grammar and punctuation

27. Which of the following correctly completes the sentence?

The capital _____ Australia is Canberra.

in	at	to	of
○	○	○	○

28. Which of the following correctly completes the sentence?

The telephone and the doorbell rang _____ the same time.

in	at	on	through
○	○	○	○

29. Shade one bubble to show where the missing comma (,) should go.

Jo likes steak chips and salad for dinner.
↑   ↑   ↑   ↑
○   ○   ○   ○

30. Which of the following correctly completes the sentence?

He _____ letters to them regularly since he was a child.

written	writes	has wrote	has written
○	○	○	○

31. Which of the following correctly completes the sentence?

The book, _____ was green, belonged to the library.

who	what	which	why
○	○	○	○

32. Which of the following correctly completes the sentence?

She _____ extremely happy since she bought that new dog.

is being	has been	was being	were being
○	○	○	○

33. Which of the following correctly completes the sentence?

I have _____ to him before.

speak	spoke	spoken	speaked
○	○	○	○

34. Which of the following correctly completes the sentence?

The use of herbs and spices in cooking _____ on the increase in Australia.

is	are	am	were
○	○	○	○

35. Which of the following correctly completes the sentence?

Jo _____ the ball just right to score six runs.

strike	striked	struck	striking
○	○	○	○

36. Which of the following correctly completes the sentences?

Karen is very tall. _____, her older brother is quite short.

So	Therefore	However	Because
○	○	○	○

37. Which sentence has the correct punctuation?

　　○ Jane, who is a tennis player, is very athletic.

　　○ Jane who, is a tennis player, is very athletic.

　　○ Jane who is a tennis player is very, athletic.

　　○ Jane who is a tennis player, is very athletic.

38. Which of the following correctly completes the sentence?

　　The movie　　　　　　already.

has begun	began	was began	have begun
○	○	○	○

39. Which of the following correctly completes the sentence?

　　This shirt button is　　　　　　smaller than this one from my coat.

more	most	much	many
○	○	○	○

40. Which of the following correctly completes the sentence?

　　There are　　　　　　students in the classroom than there are in the corridor.

lesser	fewer	few	many
○	○	○	○

41. Which one of the following is correct?

　　○ Jane didn't like salad. Neither did Jenny.

　　○ Jane didn't like salad. Or neither did Jenny.

　　○ Jane didn't like salad. Neither did not Jenny.

　　○ Jane didn't like salad. Either did Jenny.

42. Which sentence has the correct punctuation?
    - ○ The dog which, was barking, was very well trained.
    - ○ The dog which was barking was, very well trained.
    - ○ The dog, which was barking, was very well trained.
    - ○ The dog which was barking, was very well, trained.

43. Which sentence has the correct punctuation?
    - ○ He asked for it politely, so I let him have it.
    - ○ He asked "for it politely," so, I let him have it.
    - ○ He asked for "it politely" so I let him, have it.
    - ○ He asked, "for it politely, so I let him", have it.

44. Which sentence is correct?
    - ○ She and its brother went to the cinema.
    - ○ She and him went to the cinema.
    - ○ Her and his brother went to the cinema.
    - ○ She and her brother went to the cinema.

45. Shade **two** bubbles to show where the missing speech marks (" ") should go.

    ○ ↓   ○ ↓   ○ ↓   ○ ↓

    Wait a minute. It's my turn first, interrupted Jade.

46. Shade one bubble to show where the missing apostrophe (') should go.

    ○ ↓   ○ ↓   ○ ↓   ○ ↓

    Mark looked for the dogs lead so that his sisters could take the dog for a walk.

47. Which sentence has the correct punctuation?

    ○ If we are to get there at the start, what time do we have to leave.

    ○ If we are to get there at the start what time do we have to leave.

    ○ If we are to get there at the start. What time do we have to leave?

    ○ If we are to get there at the start, what time do we have to leave?

48. Which sentence is correct?

    ○ They gathered them and sort them into pairs.

    ○ They gathered them up and sorting them into pairs.

    ○ They were gathering them up and were sorted them into pairs.

    ○ They were gathering them up and sorting them into pairs.

49. Which of the following gives an instruction?

    ○ I checked to see which brand is the cheapest before I bought it.

    ○ Check to see which brand is the cheapest before you buy it.

    ○ Did you check to see which brand was cheapest before you bought it?

    ○ Checking to see which brand is cheapest before buying can save money.

50. Shade **two** bubbles to show where the missing commas (,) should go.

I enjoy eating fish and chips and I enjoy eating chocolate
⬆ ⬆ ⬆
○ ○ ○

but I wouldn't enjoy eating them together.
⬆
○

Numeracy test

This is a numeracy test. There are 40 questions to answer.

You have 45 minutes to complete the test.

You cannot use a calculator or any mathematical tools (except a ruler), but you can use pencil and paper to work out things.

The Year 5 test covers:

- Number operations (addition, subtraction, multiplication, division)
- Fractions and decimals
- Patterns and algebra
- Money and financial mathematics
- Measurement (length, area, volume, mass, time)
- Geometry (2D shapes, 3D objects)
- Data interpretation and graphs
- Basic probability
- Multi-step word problems

1.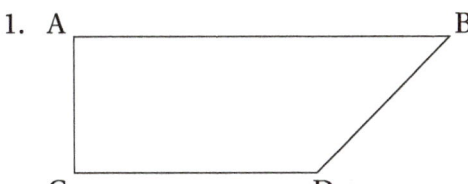

   The biggest angle in the above shape is

A	B	C	D
○	○	○	○

2. Jane folds a piece of paper in half to get a shape like the one below.

   She now cuts along the dotted line and then unfolds the paper.

   Which one of the following is the shape formed?

   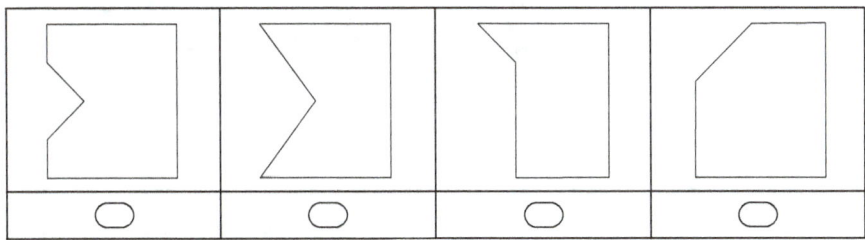

3. Which number is two thousand three hundred and nine?

239	2,039	2,390	2,309
○	○	○	○

4.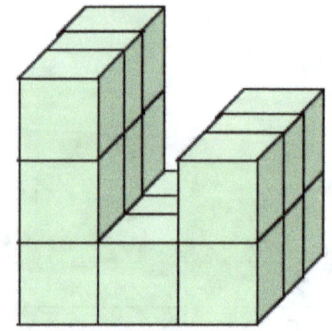

How many little cubes have been stacked to make the shape shown above?

12	15	18	20
○	○	○	○

5. Which clock shows the time 1:45?

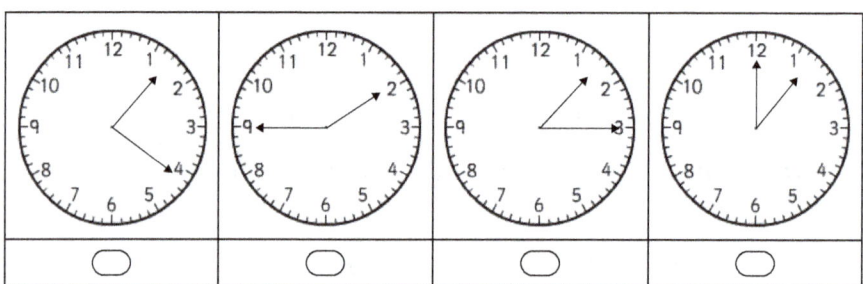

○	○	○	○

6. 4,832 ÷ 8 = ?

64	604	640	6,004
○	○	○	○

7. What is the answer when the numbers in the **triangles** are added?

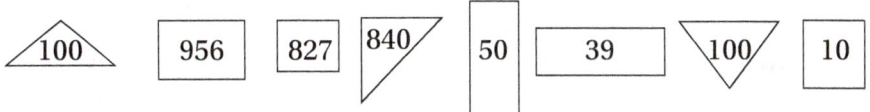

200	866	1,040	1,056
○	○	○	○

8. Matilda is 37 cm taller than Mark. If Matilda is 162 cm tall, then how tall is Mark?

125 cm	135 cm	189 cm	199 cm
○	○	○	○

9. Which one of these shapes is an octagon?

○	○	○	○

10. A Holden, a Ford and a Toyota are racing to the finish line in a car rally.

    How many different results are possible in the race?

3	6	9	12
○	○	○	○

11. What is the missing number?

$6 \times \boxed{?} = 9 \times 8$

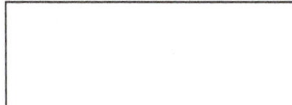

12. Find the missing number.

9	5	11	4	?
6	3	7	3	2
3	2	4	1	7

13. 5,063 can be written as

	hundreds	6	tens	3	ones

14. What does 0.2 × 30 equal?

0.06	0.6	6	60
○	○	○	○

15. When this net is made into a cube, which face will be opposite the face marked **Y**?

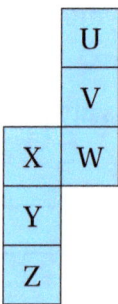

V	W	X	U
○	○	○	○

50 Year 5 Test Preparation Guide

16. Which shape could be made from the following set of faces?

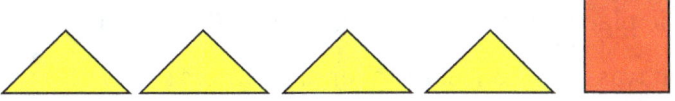

a cone	a square pyramid	a triangular pyramid	a cylinder
○	○	○	○

17. How many hundreds in 9,500?

18.

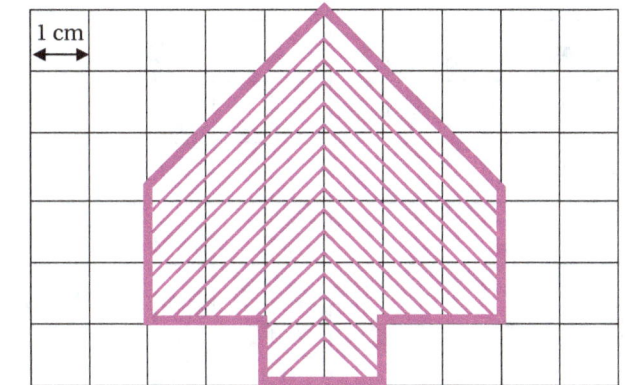

Tony drew the above shape on square centimetre graph paper.

The shaded area in square centimetres is closest to

20	21	22	23
○	○	○	○

19. Jackie had 15 counters and she gave some to Brian.

Jackie placed her counters in groups of 6 and had 2 left over.

What was the smallest number of counters she could have given to Brian?

1	2	6	7
○	○	○	○

20.

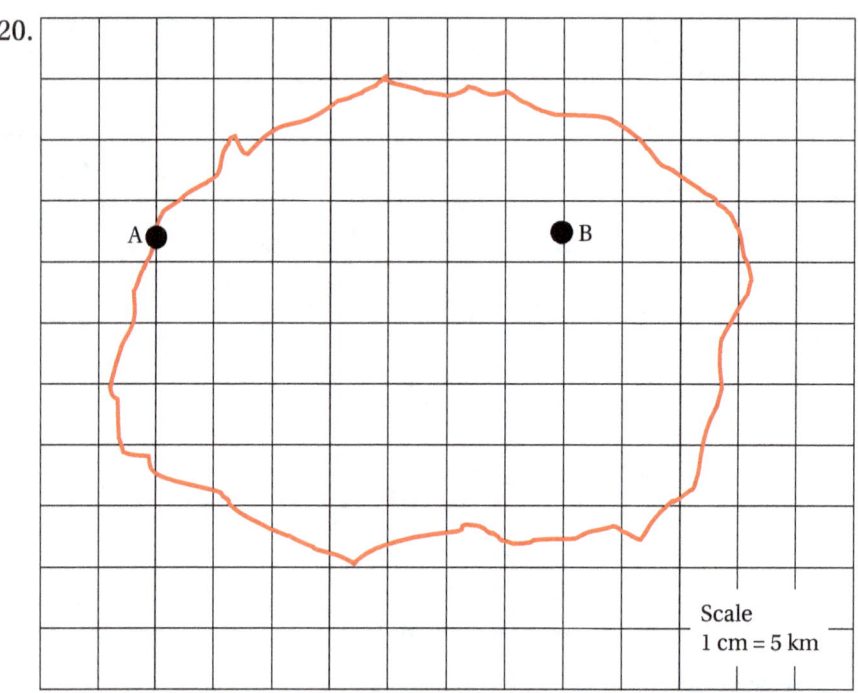

Pete the pirate finds this map of Treasure Island drawn on 1 cm graph paper. He lands at **A** and the gold he is looking for is buried at **B**.

How many kilometres must he travel from **A** to reach the gold at **B**?

21. How much change will Molly get from $10.00 if she buys a loaf of bread for $3.25 and a drink for $2.30?

$ ☐

22. Jess walked from her home to her friend's house and arrived at 4:15. If it took Jess 25 minutes to walk this distance, then what time did she leave home?

3:05	3:45	3:50	3:55
○	○	○	○

23. What fraction of the total rectangle is shaded?

24. Nina asked the Year 5 and 6 students at her school how many times a week they bought their lunch at the school tuck shop. She entered these results in the table below.

	Lunches bought at tuck shop		
	Less than 3 times a week	More than 3 times a week	Total
Grade 5	45	25	70
Grade 6	38	37	75
Total	83	62	145

How many of the students that Nina questioned bought their lunch at the tuck shop more than 3 times a week?

25	37	62	83
○	○	○	○

Numeracy test 53

25.

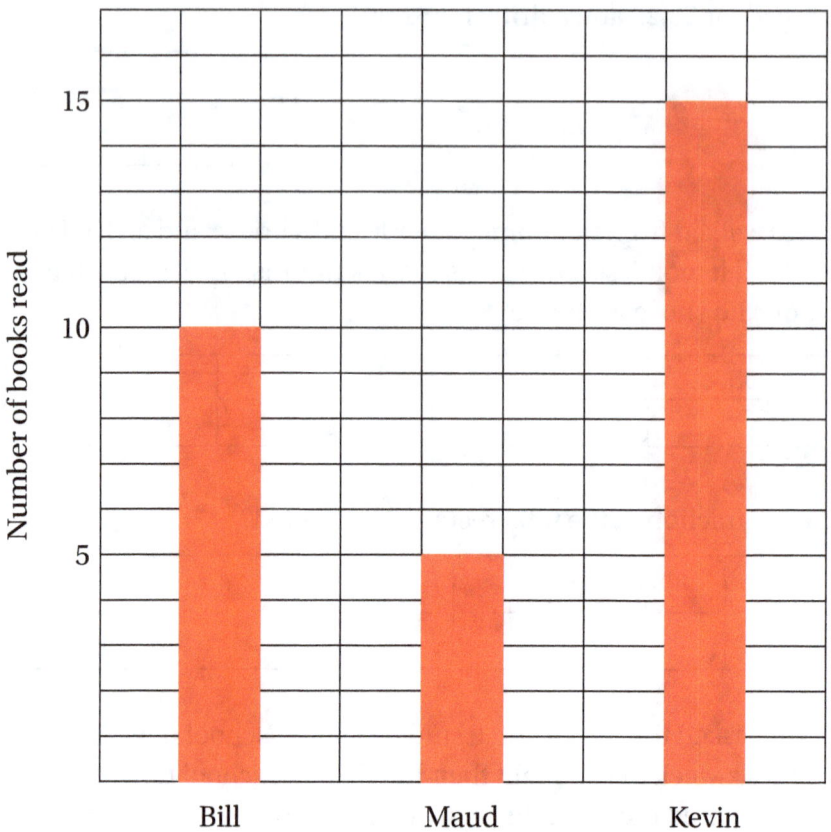

The above graph shows the number of books read by Bill, Maud and Kevin.

Which one of the following statements is true?

○ Kevin read twice the number of books that Maud read.

○ Bill and Maud together read twice the number of books that Kevin read.

○ Maud and Kevin together read twice the number of books that Bill read.

○ Bill and Maud together read more books than Kevin.

26. Find the missing number below.

563 ÷ ? = 56.3

27. Which of the following numbers is the smallest?

1	1.02	1.1	1.2
○	○	○	○

28. What is the next number in the pattern?

93 78 63 ?

29.

Harry turns the shape above a quarter of a turn in a clockwise direction.

Which one of the following would the shape now look like?

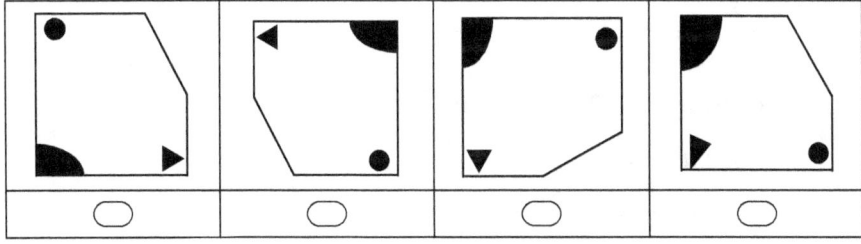

30. Which one of the following is **not** a composite number?

7	8	9	10
○	○	○	○

31. How many quarters in $5\frac{1}{4}$?

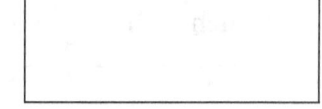

32.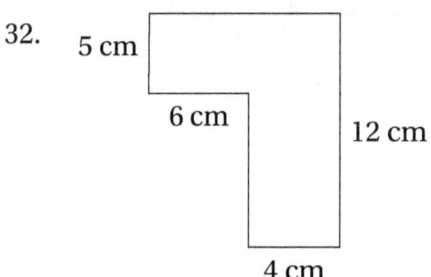

What is the perimeter of the above shape?

24 cm	27 cm	34 cm	44 cm
○	○	○	○

33. Which one of the following numbers is closest to 0.7?

0.6	0.68	0.75	0.79
○	○	○	○

34. The number 24.06 is equal to

○ 2 tens + 4 ones + 6 hundredths

○ 2 tens + 4 ones + 6 tenths

○ 2 hundreds + 4 tens + 6 hundredths

○ 2 hundreds + 4 tens + 6 tenths

35.

2 **4** **9** **8**

What is the **smallest odd number** that can be made with **three** of the above cards?

36. What is the measurement shown by the arrow?

37. A box contains 15 black marbles and 1 white marble. Josie closes her eyes and selects a marble from the box.

Which one of the following statements is true?

○ It is impossible for Josie to select a white marble.

○ It is likely that Josie will select a white marble.

○ It is unlikely that Josie will select a white marble.

○ It is certain that Josie will select a black marble.

38. Fill in the missing numbers

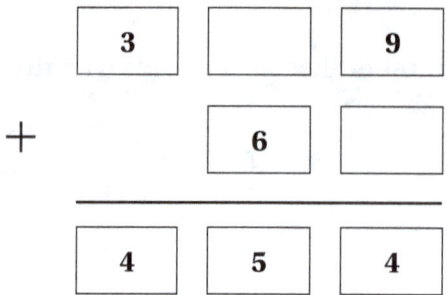

39. A bottle contains 360 ml of medicine.

    Four times each day, Meg takes a 15 ml dose of medicine.

    How many days will the medicine last?

6	14	16	24
○	○	○	○

40. The figure below is not drawn to scale.

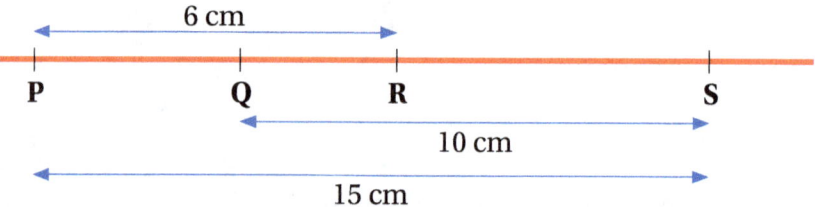

    What is the length of QR?

1 cm	4 cm	5 cm	9 cm
○	○	○	○

Answers

Writing

Here is a sample writing response for the **narrative** prompt.

The Note

The three friends, Rebecca, Raquel and Jasmine, saw the pictures of the $20, $10 and $5 notes on the notices around the school. They decided to enter the Cupcake Competition for their Twilight Sports Day next week. They had to make cupcakes at home the night before to sell during the sports. The best cakes would win prizes.

Jasmine said they could all meet at her place after school. Her mother was home then and one of the rules was that students had to make the cakes themselves, except for the butter melting and taking them out of the oven. Also, an adult had to sign a form to say the cakes were made by students.

"How will we decorate them?" asked Jasmine.

"Like Harry Potter," said Rebecca.

"No, that's old," said Raquel. "What about princesses?"

"Princesses don't have round faces," replied Jasmine. "What about netballs?"

Netball was her favourite sport.

"No way!" yelled Rebecca and Raquel.

"What do you think, Mum?"

Jasmine's mother said the simpler, the better and to use colours.

"A rainbow!" said the three girls together.

They had to follow the recipe on the form. Raquel was good at Maths, so she measured three-quarters of a cup for the milk and sugar and, after a while, knew where to cut the margarine for 125 grams. Rebecca and Jasmine did the mixing. Because they couldn't divide the bowl into three, Jasmine's little brother was allowed to lick the bowl and the icing container. They used only four icing colours, instead of seven, to keep the lines straight. When they put the two rows of cakes in a curve on the cardboard, it really looked like a rainbow.

The announcement came at lunchtime. First prize went to the students who had made vampire cakes, second prize was for butterfly cakes and third prize was for rainbow cakes. Rebecca, Raquel and Jasmine did high fives.

After the sports the three friends went up to the principal to receive their money. Inside the envelope was $5 with "To the 3rd place winner in the Cupcake Competition" on it.

The principal said that Raquel had to work out how to divide it into three but she wasn't allowed to use a ruler and scissors.

Lots of parents thought she was funny.

Here is a sample writing response for the **Persuasive** prompt.

A cat makes a better pet than a dog

Our cat is cuddly, quiet and pretty, so it is a much better pet than a dog.

Sometimes our cat will sleep on my bed at night. She is very warm and keeps very still. When my little brother is tired he lies down with his head on the cat's silky fur and snuggles into her. Often, when we are watching TV our cat will be sitting with us on the couch. She doesn't really watch TV but she enjoys our company. You can't get a dog that would do any of those things so, for us, a cat makes a better pet than a dog.

Our cat doesn't make any noise. She purrs when she's asleep and that's about all. We do know when she is eating but I think that it's the dry food causing the sound, not really the cat. For people who don't like loud, sudden interruptions, a cat is a much better pet than a dog.

I like to put ribbons on our cat. They make her look pretty and I can change them during the year. She wears the colours of my football team during the finals, and red and green at Christmas time. I think that a dog would look silly in ribbons but they suit our cat's cute, little face.

Because of what our cat does, looks like and the fact that she is quiet make her a much better pet than a dog.

Reading

The ant and the dove

1. **What word could be used to describe the bank of the river instead of *slick*?**

    ○ dry

    ● slippery

    ○ sticky

    ○ grassy

    Slippery *is the correct answer. We can tell the bank was 'slippery' because the ant slipped into the river.*

2. **What word best describes the dove in this story?**

    ○ coward

    ● hero

    ○ bully

    ○ tease

    Hero *is the best answer because the dove saved the ant from drowning. Coward, bully and tease do not fit well as answers.*

3. **Why did the ant bite the man on the toe?**

    ○ the man made the ant fall in the river

    ○ the ant was afraid

    ○ the ant did not like people

    ● the ant wanted to save the dove

    The ant wanted to save the dove *is the best answer. The story tells us that the ant bit the man on the toe when the ant saw that the man was trying to hurt the dove.*

4. **In the beginning of the story, what word could best be used in place of *parched*?**

    ○ angry
    ○ refreshed
    ● thirsty
    ○ cool

   Thirsty is the correct answer. From the story, we can tell that parched can mean thirsty. The first sentence tells us that the ant was parched and the next sentence in the story tells us that the ant bent down to get a drink.

5. **In the story, the ant is '*floundering for his life*'. This means the ant is**

    ○ running for his life
    ○ fighting with the dove
    ○ fighting with the man
    ● trying not to drown

   Trying not to drown is the correct answer. The ant cannot be running, or fighting with the dove or the man, because the ant is in the water.

6. **What do you think is the message to be taken from this story?**

    ● kind acts are repaid
    ○ ants can drown
    ○ men do not like doves
    ○ that rivers are dangerous

   Kind acts are repaid is the best answer because the most important part of the story is that the dove saves the ant, which is a kind act, and the ant then saves the dove in return.

Orangutan

7. **The text describes orangutans as *arboreal*. This means that orangutans**
   - ○ live in caves
   - ○ live in captivity
   - ● live in trees
   - ○ are not real

   Live in trees is the correct answer. The text states that 'Orangutans are arboreal, which means that they live in trees...'

8. **Male orangutans**
   - ○ live in groups
   - ○ stay in the trees
   - ● like to be alone
   - ○ weigh about 100 kilograms

   Like to be alone is the correct answer. The text states that 'males are largely solitary creatures.' Solitary means alone.

9. **Orangutans are an *endangered* species. This means that orangutans**
   - ○ are dangerous
   - ○ are kept in captivity
   - ● are in danger
   - ○ are lonely

   Are in danger is the correct answer. The text tells us that they are 'endangered because their habitats are being destroyed and because they have been hunted and sold as pets'. Also, the other answers are not appropriate.

10. **In Sumatra and Kalimantan some orangutans are kept in rehabilitation centres. They are kept in these centres**
    - ○ to be sold later as pets
    - ○ to learn to be nomadic
    - ● to learn survival skills
    - ○ to protect humans

    To learn survival skills *is the correct answer. The text tells us that orang utans kept in rehabilitation centres 'are taught the skills they need to survive in the wild'.*

11. **Orangutans do *not* eat**
    - ○ leaves
    - ○ birds' eggs
    - ○ insects
    - ● birds

    Birds *is the correct answer. The text tells us that orangutans like to eat leaves, birds' eggs and insects. 'Birds' eggs' means the eggs of birds and not the birds themselves.*

12. **Which of the following statements about orangutans is *incorrect***
    - ○ males usually weigh more than females
    - ○ females usually stay up in the trees
    - ○ they only have one enemy
    - ● females usually give birth to more than one young

    Females usually give birth to more than one young *is the incorrect statement. The text tells us that they usually give birth to only 'one, but sometimes two, young'.*

Australian drought

13. **Where does grey water come from?**

    ○ taps

    ○ rainwater tanks

    ● washing machines

    ○ gutters

    Washing machines *is the correct answer. Patty's letter tells us this when she states in the second paragraph that people should be using 'grey water from their washing machines'.*

14. **Which of the following do the two writers disagree on?**

    ○ water needs to be conserved

    ● the Government is doing enough

    ○ the environment is precious

    ○ rainwater tanks help in a drought

    The Government is doing enough *is the correct answer. Patty states in her letter that she doesn't think the Government is doing enough. Bill's responding letter argues that the Government has 'put plenty of restrictions on the use of water', and that people who buy water tanks 'can claim money bank from the Government'. Both these arguments suggest that Bill disagrees with Patty and believes that the Government is doing enough. Also, Bill clearly agrees with Patty on the other points.*

15. **Bill writes that the Government has '*put plenty of restrictions on the use of water*'. Why does he write this?**

    ○ he agrees with Patty

    ○ he works for the government

    ● he disagrees with Patty

    ○ he thinks that Australians are water 'Wallys'

He disagrees with Patty *is the correct answer. Bill's letter is a response to Patty's letter and his comments on the Government are made to show that he disagrees with Patty in her argument that the Government is not doing enough.*

16. **Why does Patty think that water tanks are a great idea?**
    - ○ so people will use less grey water
    - ○ so people will use more tap water
    - ○ so people can get money back from the Government
    - ● so people will use more rainwater

So people will use more rainwater *is the correct answer. The answers referring to the use of grey water and tap water are both completely incorrect. Only Bill notes that people can claim money from the Government for buying water tanks. Patty does not discuss this point.*

17. **What does Patty's letter tell us about Patty?**
    - ○ she likes the Government
    - ● she cares for the environment
    - ○ she cares for Bill
    - ○ she is not a farmer

She cares for the environment *is the correct answer. Patty's letter does not indicate that she likes the Government, and it does not state that she is, or is not, a farmer. Also, Patty's letter was written before Bill's responding letter, suggesting that she did not know Bill at the time she wrote her letter.*

18. **What type of letter is Bill's?**
    - ○ a comment
    - ○ an instruction
    - ● a response
    - ○ a list

A response is the best answer. In the first sentence, Bill's letter states that he agrees with Patty's letter on a number of points, therefore Bill's letter is written as an answer, or response, to Patty's letter.

Eggs

19. **Why would Thomas have gone up to the chook shed instead of the house?**

    ○ to get out of the sun

    ● because his dad wouldn't catch him stealing eggs from there

    ○ to hide from the narrator

    ○ for extra eggs

    Because his dad wouldn't catch him stealing eggs from there is the correct answer. In the text, the narrator states 'Thomas wouldn't have gone inside for the eggs if his dad was awake, he would have snuck up back to the chook shed instead'. This suggests that Thomas does not want to be caught stealing eggs by his dad and explains why Thomas would have gone to the chook shed instead.

20. **What does the narrator mean by the sentence '*...It will get hot enough*'?**

    The narrator means that the sun will heat the tin enough to cook the eggs.

21. **'*...their clear jelly bodies start to turn a wispy, milky white...*' What does this mean?**

    ○ Thomas and the narrator are turning white

    ○ the sun is going down

    ● the eggs are cooking

    ○ the eggs are rotten

The eggs are cooking is the correct answer. The 'clear jelly bodies' is a reference to the eggs, which turn white when they are cooked.

22. **In the story, Thomas' dad did a late shift the night before, so Thomas thinks he has until at least three o'clock before he has to go in. This suggests that Thomas**

    ○ needs to go in before the sun goes down
    ● needs to go in before his dad wakes up
    ○ knows that his dad will not be angry
    ○ will get into trouble if he goes to the chook shed

    Needs to go in before his dad wakes up *is the best answer. In the text, Thomas is guessing that his dad will sleep until at least three because he worked late the night before.*

23. **What kind of word *best* describes the relationship between Thomas and the narrator?**

    ○ brothers
    ○ enemies
    ● friends
    ○ cousins

    Friends *is the best answer. If Thomas and the narrator were brothers, the narrator would call the man in the story 'Dad' and not 'Thomas' dad'. If the boys in this story were cousins, Thomas' dad would be an uncle to the narrator. The text does not suggest this and the boys are obviously not enemies.*

24. **Why do you think the narrator laughs when Thomas shows off his burnt finger?**

    ○ because he is hot

    ○ because he wants Thomas to be hurt

    ○ because he doesn't like Thomas

    ● because he is amazed

    Because he is amazed is the best answer. The narrator laughs in response to what he is being shown because he finds it hard to believe.

Water baby

25. **When the starting gun went off, Shane *cut the water like a knife*. This means that Shane**

    ○ used a knife to cut the water

    ○ dove into the water roughly

    ● went through the water sharply

    ○ swam very slowly

    Went through the water sharply is the correct answer. From reading the text we can tell that Shane did not use an actual knife to cut the water, nor did she dive roughly or swim slowly.

26. **The text states that Shane 'gave herself over to competitive swimming'. This means that she**

    ○ gave up going to school

    ○ gave up her diet

    ○ brought herself over to the swimming pool

    ● gave up other activities for swimming

    Gave up other activities for swimming is the correct answer. In the same sentence, the text states that Shane 'gave up all other interests and gave herself over to competitive swimming'.

27. **Shane swam open-eyed underwater**
    - ○ during bathtime
    - ● by age three
    - ○ while snorkelling
    - ○ by age five

    By age three *is the correct answer. The text states: 'Before she was three she could swim underwater at the pool with her eyes open.'*

28. **The main purpose of this text is to**
    - ○ instruct
    - ○ criticise
    - ○ argue
    - ● inform

    Inform *is the correct answer. The text tells us about Shane Gould and her swimming career. It does not criticise or argue or instruct.*

29. **Which quote from the text best shows that Shane was very determined to succeed?**
    - ○ 'she knew her gift for swimming was special'
    - ○ 'she was so confident she'd win'
    - ● 'her persistence and single-mindedness paid off'
    - ○ 'she loved the water from babyhood'

    Her persistence and single-mindedness paid off *is the best answer. In this context, 'persistence and single-mindedness' have the same meaning as 'very determined'.*

30. **Why did Shane ask for her braces to be removed before the Olympics?**

    ○ because they were slowing her down

    ● because she was confident she was going to win

    ○ because she didn't like her photo being taken

    ○ because she was persistent

Because she was confident she was going to win is the best answer. The text states: '...she was so confident that she'd win gold at the Games that she asked her parents if she could have her braces removed just for the competition.'

Elephants

31. **How do other animals in the ecosystem rely on elephants?**

    ○ for protection

    ● as a water source

    ○ as a provider of food

    ○ for shelter

As a water source is the correct answer. The text explains that elephants living in dry environments use their tusks to dig water holes that are often the only source of water for other animals.

32. **Using information in the text, what is *a matriarchal group* likely to mean?**

A matriarchal group is a group of females led by an elder female.

This information is contained within the text: 'Female elephants live in matriarchal groups in which one elder female is the leader.'

33. **Asian and African elephants have very different technical names: *Elephas maximus* and *Loxodonta africana*. Why is this?**

    - they are different species
    ○ they live on different sides of the world
    ○ they are not similar in any way
    ○ because African elephants are bigger

    They are different species *is the best answer. The text tells us: 'There are only two species of elephant left: the Asian elephant (Elephas maximus) and the African elephant (Loxodonta africana).' We can tell therefore, that these special names are given to each species. The names are different because the species are different.*

34. **From reading the text, we can tell that *herbivores***

    ○ are *Loxodonta africana*
    - do not eat meat
    ○ have *tushes*
    ○ give birth to a single calf

    Do not eat meat *is the best answer. The text explains that elephants are herbivores that eat all kinds of vegetation. From this, we can guess that they do not eat meat.*

35. **What are some of the features of the Asian Elephant?**

    All of the following are correct answers: *Asian elephants have a large, domed head and much smaller ears than the African elephant. Asian elephants are smaller than African elephants. Only male Asian elephants have tusks. Some female Asian elephants have tushes.*

Language conventions

Spelling

The spelling mistakes in these sentences have been circled. Write the correct spelling for each circled word in the box.

1. Jenna went (shoping) today.

   shopping

2. We waited (abowt) an hour for the bus.

   about

3. He used a ruler to (mesure).

   measure

4. Liz cut out the picture with her (sizzors).

   scissors

5. Possums like eating (froot).

   fruit

6. Everyone thinks Anna is (pritty).

   pretty

7. Brendon loves Vegemite (samwiches).

   sandwiches

8. Peter was (greatful) for his birthday present.

grateful

9. Mrs Hartley is a good (teecher.)

teacher

10. Mum cooked a (sosage) on the barbecue.

sausage

The spelling mistakes on these labels have been circled. Write the correct spelling for each circled word in the box.

11. (cumputer) screen

computer

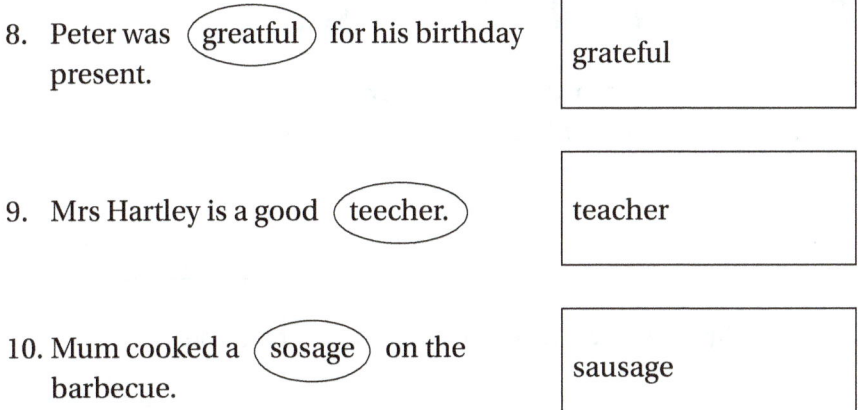

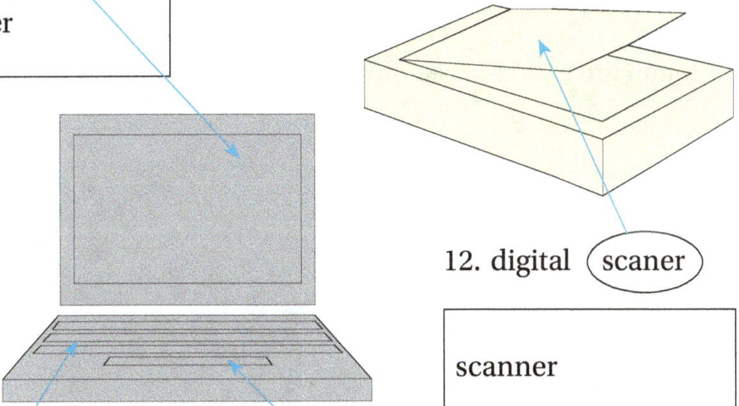

12. digital (scaner)

scanner

13. (keybord) controls

keyboard

14. (mows) pad

mouse

Answers 75

Read the text about *The visit*.

**Each line has one word that is incorrect.
Write the correct spelling of the word in the box.**

The visit

15. My parrents have been waiting | parents

16. a very long time for my unkle to | uncle

17. visit us. They allways talk about him | always

18. and are exited to see him again. | excited

**Each sentence has one word that is incorrect.
Write the correct spelling of the word in the box.**

19. We need to show caushun when crossing the road.

caution

20. I am very good at rapping presents.

wrapping

21. My grandmother owns an expensive cristal ball.

crystal

22. The art galery has many famous paintings.

gallery

23. John claims he has the bigest feet in the school.

biggest

24. The tourist lost his luggidge at the airport.

luggage

25. Too much moishture in a home can cause mould.

moisture

26. The mountain's summit was at a great hite.

height

Grammar and punctuation

27. Which of the following correctly completes the sentence?

The capital _____ Australia is Canberra.

in	at	to	of
○	○	○	●

28. Which of the following correctly completes the sentence?

The telephone and the doorbell rang _____ the same time.

in	at	on	through
○	●	○	○

29. Shade one bubble to show where the missing comma (,) should go.

Jo likes steak chips and salad for dinner.
  ↑   ↑   ↑   ↑
  ○   ●   ○   ○

30. Which of the following correctly completes the sentence?

He _____ letters to them regularly since he was a child.

written	writes	has wrote	has written
○	○	○	●

31. Which of the following correctly completes the sentence?

The book, _____ was green, belonged to the library.

who	what	which	why
○	○	●	○

32. Which of the following correctly completes the sentence?

She _____ extremely happy since she bought that new dog.

is being	has been	was being	were being
○	●	○	○

33. Which of the following correctly completes the sentence?

I have _____ to him before.

speak	spoke	spoken	speaked
○	○	●	○

34. Which of the following correctly completes the sentence?

The use of herbs and spices in cooking _____ on the increase in Australia.

is	are	am	were
●	○	○	○

35. Which of the following correctly completes the sentence?

Jo _____ the ball just right to score six runs.

strike	striked	struck	striking
○	○	●	○

36. Which of the following correctly completes the sentences?

Karen is very tall. _____, her older brother is quite short.

So	Therefore	However	Because
○	○	●	○

37. Which sentence has the correct punctuation?

- ● Jane, who is a tennis player, is very athletic.
- ○ Jane who, is a tennis player, is very athletic.
- ○ Jane who is a tennis player is very, athletic.
- ○ Jane who is a tennis player, is very athletic.

38. Which of the following correctly completes the sentence?

The movie _____ already.

has begun	began	was began	have begun
●	○	○	○

39. Which of the following correctly completes the sentence?

This shirt button is _____ smaller than this one from my coat.

more	most	much	many
○	○	●	○

40. Which of the following correctly completes the sentence?

There are _____ students in the classroom than there are in the corridor.

lesser	fewer	few	many
○	●	○	○

41. Which one of the following is correct?

- ● Jane didn't like salad. Neither did Jenny.
- ○ Jane didn't like salad. Or neither did Jenny.
- ○ Jane didn't like salad. Neither did not Jenny.
- ○ Jane didn't like salad. Either did Jenny.

42. Which sentence has the correct punctuation?

　　○ The dog which, was barking, was very well trained.
　　○ The dog which was barking was, very well trained.
　　● The dog, which was barking, was very well trained.
　　○ The dog which was barking, was very well, trained.

43. Which sentence has the correct punctuation?

　　● He asked for it politely, so I let him have it.
　　○ He asked "for it politely," so, I let him have it.
　　○ He asked for "it politely" so I let him, have it.
　　○ He asked, "for it politely, so I let him", have it.

44. Which sentence is correct?

　　○ She and its brother went to the cinema.
　　○ She and him went to the cinema.
　　○ Her and his brother went to the cinema.
　　● She and her brother went to the cinema.

45. Shade **two** bubbles to show where the missing speech marks (" ") should go.

　　● ○ ● ○

　　Wait a minute. It's my turn first, interrupted Jade.

46. Shade one bubble to show where the missing apostrophe (') should go.

　　○ ● ○ ○

Mark looked for the dogs lead so that his sisters could take the dog for a walk.

47. Which sentence has the correct punctuation?

   ○ If we are to get there at the start, what time do we have to leave.

   ○ If we are to get there at the start what time do we have to leave.

   ○ If we are to get there at the start. What time do we have to leave?

   ● If we are to get there at the start, what time do we have to leave?

48. Which sentence is correct?

   ○ They gathered them and sort them into pairs.

   ○ They gathered them up and sorting them into pairs.

   ○ They were gathering them up and were sorted them into pairs.

   ● They were gathering them up and sorting them into pairs.

49. Which of the following gives an instruction?

   ○ I checked to see which brand is the cheapest before I bought it.

   ● Check to see which brand is the cheapest before you buy it.

   ○ Did you check to see which brand was cheapest before you bought it?

   ○ Checking to see which brand is cheapest before buying can save money.

50. Shade **two** bubbles to show where the missing commas (,) should go.

I enjoy eating fish and chips and I enjoy eating chocolate
○　　　　　　●　　　　　　●

but I wouldn't enjoy eating them together.
○

Language conventions answers in detail

Questions 1–26 are spellings, so their answers are self-evident.

Question 27: The only appropriate preposition in Standard English is *of*.

Question 28: The only appropriate preposition in Standard English is *at*.

Question 29: The comma comes after 'steak' because it is a list. It is not appropriate anywhere else because as a simple sentence it contains a single clause.

Question 30: The sentence demands the past tense, so the answer cannot be 'writes'. The past tense is 'wrote' and cannot be used as the past participle to form the perfect aspect, so the answer cannot be 'have wrote'. The past participle 'written' requires an auxiliary verb 'has', so this cannot be the answer; therefore, the perfect past tense 'has written' is the only possible answer. The perfect aspect implies that the action happened or began in a previous period of time indicated by the conjunction 'since'.

Question 31: A relative pronoun is required here, so 'what' and 'why' (interrogative pronouns) cannot be used, and 'who' is used to refer to people, so 'which' is the only correct answer.

Question 32: The past perfect tense 'has been' is required. 'Was being' and 'were being' are past progressive, 'is being' is present tense. The perfect aspect implies that the action happened or began in a previous period of time indicated by the conjunction 'since'.

Question 33: The past participle 'spoken' is required with the auxiliary verb 'have'. 'Spoke' never takes an auxiliary verb, 'spoked' is not the correct past tense, and 'speak', is present tense.

Question 34: This is subject-verb agreement. 'The use' is the noun phrase (post-modified with 'of herbs and spices'). It is third person singular and must therefore take the verb 'is'. 'Am' is first person; 'are' and 'were' are either second person or third person plural.

Question 35: 'Struck' is the past tense of the irregular verb 'strike', not 'striked'. The sentence demanded a past tense and so could not use the present tense 'strike' or the gerund 'striking'.

Question 36: 'So', 'because' and 'therefore' all suggest cause and effect, and it would be unusual to find a subordinating conjunction to connect these two clauses as neither clause is subordinate. The adverbial 'however' allows the second clause to modify the content of the first clause.

Question 37: 'Who is a tennis player' is the relative clause that has been embedded in the main clause 'Jane is very athletic', and so therefore needs surrounding by the commas.

Question 38: The sentence requires the perfect tense, requiring the appropriate form of the auxiliary 'to have' and the past participle of 'begin', which is 'begun'. 'Began' is the simple past tense, and 'was begun' is the past progressive, so these answers are inappropriate. 'Movie' is singular so requires 'has' as the auxiliary, thus: 'The movie has begun already' is the correct answer.

Question 39: The answer cannot be 'more' or 'most' because 'smaller' is a comparative. 'Many' is an adjective suggesting quantity. 'Much' is an adverbial intensifier that modifies the comparative adjective 'smaller'.

Question 40: The only comparative adjective that is appropriate in Standard English is 'fewer'.

Question 41: 'Jane didn't like salad. Neither did Jenny' is the correct answer because the negative 'neither' corresponds to the negative 'didn't'.

Question 42: 'The dog, which was barking, was very well trained' is correct because the relative clause that gives more information about the noun phrase is separated by commas.

Question 43: There is no speech directly reported in this sentence, so there is no need for speech marks. The only sentence without speech marks is: 'He asked for it politely, so I let him have it.'

Question 44: The sentence requires the subject pronoun 'she' as 'she' is the subject of the sentence. 'Her' is the possessive pronoun that suggests the brother belongs to 'she'. (Technically, this is not strictly speaking a possessive pronoun, but rather functions as a possessive adjective to modify the word 'brother'.)

Question 45: The full utterance being reported is: 'Wait a minute. It's my turn first'; therefore, inverted commas (" ") need to be place either side of this utterance.

Question 46: The lead belongs grammatically to the dog, and so requires a singular possessive inflection: 's.

Question 47: The sentence is interrogative (question), so therefore needs a question mark. The statement demands a single sentence of two clauses, therefore, only one full stop.

Question 48: The verb tenses and aspects have to agree in a compound sentence. The use of the past progressive tense 'were gathering' in the first clause requires the need of the gerund 'sorting' in the second clause. Also, the gerund or present tense cannot be used in the second clause if the simple past had been used in the first.

Question 49: 'Check to see which brand is the cheapest before you buy it' is the imperative sentence (command) which can be identified because it begins with the verb element of the sentence.

Question 50: The commas are used to separate the clause elements. The first one comes before the coordinating conjunction 'and', and the second one before the conjunction 'but'. (The first conjunction 'and' does not coordinate clauses, but rather is used to list.)

Numeracy

1. A and C are each 90°. B is acute, D is obtuse. Hence, **D is the largest angle**.

2. When you open the paper you will get an indented triangular shape which will not start at the bottom of the rectangle. **Hence, the shape on the left in the answers.**

3. 2 thousands 3 hundreds 0 tens and 9 ones = **2,309**

4. 6 in right-hand section + 3 in middle section + 9 in left-hand section = **18**

5. 1:45 is a quarter to 2. The little hand has almost reached 2 and the big hand is on the 9. **The second clock from the left in the answers.**

6. 8 divides into 48 hundred 6 hundred, 8 divides into 3 tens 0 tens and 3 tens = 30 ones over, 30 ones + 2 ones = 32 ones. 8 divides into 32 ones 4 ones. Answer is 6 hundred 0 tens and 4 ones = **604**

7. △ is a triangle.

   Numbers in the triangles added = 100 + 840 + 100 = **1,040**

8. Mark is 37 cm shorter than Matilda. 162 – 37 = **125 cm**

9. An octagon has 8 sides, so **the third answer from the left**.

10. HFT, HTF, THF, TFH, FHT, FTH = **6**

11. 9 × 8 = 72, 6 × 12 = 72, so missing number is **12**

12. The number at the top of each column is the sum of the two numbers under it.

    7 + 2 = **9**

13. 5 thousands is **50** hundreds

14. 0.2 × 30 = 0.2 × 3 × 10 = 0.6 × 10 = **6**

15. W will be the base, X will come up the side and Y and Z will wrap around to make sides so that Z is opposite X, and **V is opposite Y**. U will be the top opposite W.

16. A square base with a triangle on each side of the base slanting to meet at a vertex at the top. **This is a square pyramid.**

17. This is 9 thousands and 5 hundreds. There are 10 hundreds in a thousand, so 90 hundreds in 9 thousands + the 5 hundreds = **95** hundreds

18. There are 20 full squares and 6 half squares. 2 halves make a whole square so 6 halves = 3 squares. 20 + 3 = **23**

19. Jackie could make 1 or 2 groups of 6. To give the least number of counters to Brian she needs to make the most groups i.e. 2. 2 groups of 6 = 12 and 2 left over makes 14 so she would have given **1** counter to Brian.

20. Distance from A to B on map = 7 cm. Scale is 1 cm = 5 km.

    Hence, 7 cm = 7 × 5 = **35 km**

21. Bread and drink cost $3.25 + $2.30 = $5.55.
    Change = $10.00 − $5.55 = **$4.45**

22. 25 minutes before 4:15 is 10 minutes before 4:00 i.e. **3:50**

23. 3 of the total 8 small rectangles is shaded, so $\frac{3}{8}$

24. The total in the column for more than 3 times a week, i.e. **62**

25. Bill read 10 books, Maud read 5 books and Kevin read 15 books. Maud and Kevin together read 20 books. **Maud and Kevin together read twice the number of books that Bill read.**

26. 563 ÷ **10** = 56.3

27. **1** is the smallest. All the other numbers have a bit added onto 1.

28. Each number is 15 less than the previous number. 63 − 15 = **48**

29. Turning this shape the way a clock hand turns, i.e. to the right for a quarter of a turn would give **the first picture on the left**.

30. A composite number has factors other than itself and 1. 8 and 10 have a factor of 2 and 9 has a factor of 3 so they are composite numbers. **7** only has factors 7 and 1 so it is not a composite number.

31. There are 4 quarters in 1, so 20 quarters in 5 so **21** quarters in $5\frac{1}{4}$

32. Perimeter = 5 + 10 + 12 + 4 + 7 + 6 = **44 cm**

33. **0.68** is closest to 0.7

    0.6 is 0.1 less than 0.7, 0.68 is 0.02 less than 0.7,
    0.75 is 0.05 greater than 0.7, 0.79 is 0.09 greater than 0.7

34. 24.06 is 2 tens 4 ones 0 tenths and 6 hundredths

    = **2 tens + 4 ones + 6 hundredths**

35. To be odd it must have the 9 in the ones column. To be smallest it must have the smallest number, 2 in the hundreds column and the next smallest number, 4 in the tens column. This gives **249**

36. Each small mark represents 0.2 Three marks past 13 gives **13.6**

37. It is possible but not likely for Josie to get a white marble since there is one white marble in the box. Hence, it is not certain she will get a black one. The true statement is that **it is unlikely that Josie will select a white marble**.

38. The number added to 9 to give a 4 in the answer must be **5**. 9 + 5 = 14. Carry the 1 ten to the tens column to get 1 + 6 = 7 and add **8** to this to get a 5 in the answer in the tens column.

39. 4 lots of 15 ml doses = 60 ml per day.

    360 ml split into 60 ml days = 360 ÷ 60

    = 360 ÷ 6 ÷ 10 = 60 ÷ 10 = **6 days**

40. PQ = 15 − 10 = 5. QR = 6 − 5 = **1 cm**

www.ingramcontent.com/pod-product-compliance
Lightning Source LLC
Chambersburg PA
CBHW070313120526
44590CB00017B/2660